3

I wash when I get up.

4

Wash, Wash, Wash

Written by Gill Budgell

Illustrated by Iva Sasheva

Collins

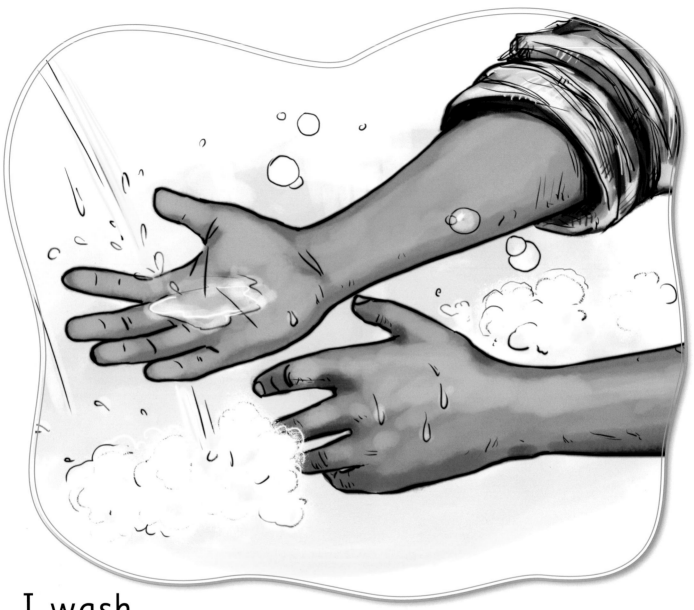

I wash.

2

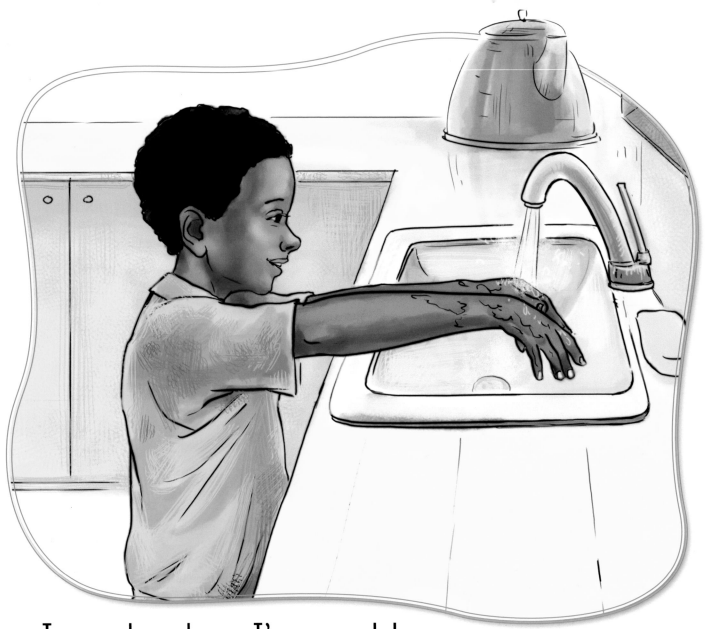

I wash when I'm muddy.

I wash when I eat.

I wash when I'm messy.

I wash when I go to bed.

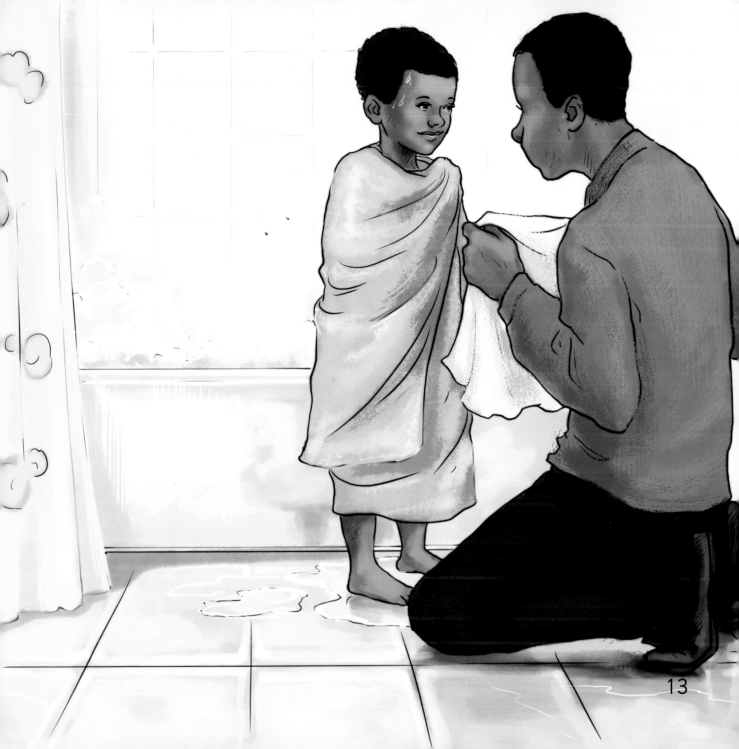

I wash

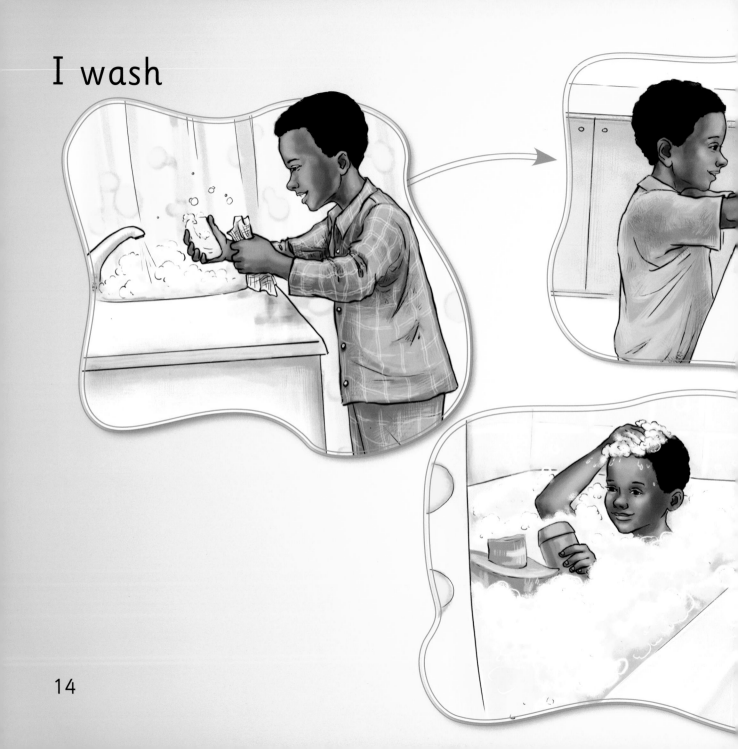

14

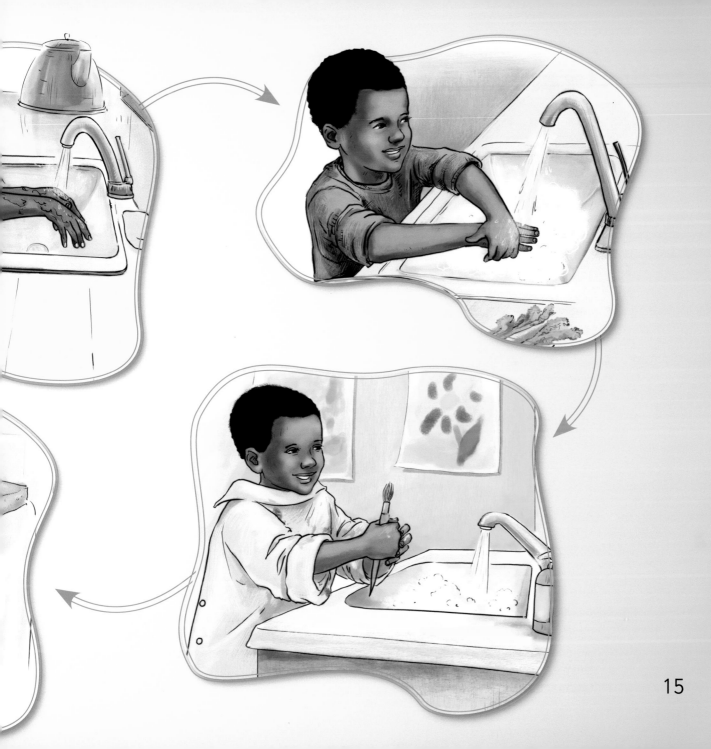

Ideas for reading

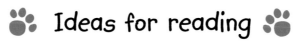

Written by Clare Dowdall, PhD
Lecturer and Primary Literacy Consultant

Learning objectives: children read and understand simple sentences; they demonstrate understanding when talking with others about what they have read; they manage their own basic hygiene and personal needs successfully; they talk about the features of their own immediate environment and how environments might vary from one another

Curriculum links: Physical development: Health and self-care

High frequency words: I, get, up, go, to

Interest words: wash, muddy, messy

Resources: soap, handwash, whiteboard, cards containing words from the book

Word count: 30

Getting started

- Read the title together. Ask children to describe what the boys on the front cover are doing.

- Challenge children to read the blurb aloud. Help them to read the word *when* fluently. Ask children to answer the boy's question, *When do I wash?* Help them to suggest when he might wash and why it's important to wash. Ask children when they last washed and why.

- Explain that this is an information book that will tell us when the boy washes. Ask children to suggest different times of day when he might wash, and why. Add their suggestions to the whiteboard.

Reading and responding

- Read pp2–3. Model how to describe what is happening in the pictures, introducing new vocabulary and wondering aloud, e.g. *the boy is washing his hands ... I think his brother is going to help him to dry them on the towel ...*

- Turn to pp4–5. Model how to read the text, *I wash when I get up.* Ask children to practise reading this sentence aloud. Ask them to read the words and discuss the pictures with a partner. Question the children to extend their thinking and understanding.